The Reagan Way

The
Reagan
Way

JEFFREY MORRIS

LERNER PUBLICATIONS COMPANY
MINNEAPOLIS

To Mat and Jennie, Josh and Ben
Who set the standard for friendship

Library of Congress Cataloging-in-Publication Data

Morris, Jeffrey Brandon, 1941-
    The Reagan way / by Jeffrey B. Morris.
      p. cm. — (Great presidential decisions)
    Includes index.
    ISBN 0-8225-2931-9
    1. Reagan, Ronald—Juvenile literature. 2. United States—
Politics and government—1981-1989—Decision making—
Juvenile literature. [1. Reagan, Ronald. 2. United States—
Politics and government—1981-1989. 3. Decision making.]
I. Title. II. Series.
E877.M67 1996
973.927'092—dc20   94-24644
                                                            CIP
                                                             AC

Manufactured in the United States of America
1 2 3 4 5 6 - JR - 01 00 99 98 97 96

Contents

Introduction

*T*HE AMERICANS WHO WROTE THE Constitution of the United States faced an unusual opportunity. They wanted to give American presidents enough power to make important decisions but not enough power to become a monarch. They wanted to protect the rights of citizens by limiting the power of the president.

Their country had won independence from Great Britain, which had a monarchical government. Most European nations at that time were governed by monarchies—by kings and queens. But Americans wanted a republic, a form of government in which power resides with those citizens who are entitled to vote. The government is run by elected officers and representatives who are responsible to the citizenry and who govern according to law.

The signing of the Constitution, presented here by artist Thomas Rossiter, took place on September 17, 1787, at the Pennsylvania State House (now called Independence Hall) in Philadelphia, Pennsylvania.

The framers of the United States Constitution wanted a government powerful enough to protect the country from foreign enemies, but not powerful enough to take away the rights of the citizens. To accomplish this goal, they created a complex form of government. The framers divided the powers of the new government among three branches. They thought that the least powerful branch would be the judiciary. That branch was supposed to hear and decide lawsuits, decide disputes between the U.S. government and individual states, and keep the other two branches within their constitutional powers.

The framers expected the legislative branch, the Senate and the House of Representatives, to be the most powerful. Congress was supposed to make laws, levy taxes, and choose how to spend money.

The framers of the Constitution had the most trouble agreeing on the powers of the executive branch. The head of that branch is the president. The framers wanted a president who could act speedily and forcefully. On the other hand, they definitely did not want someone with the powers of a king or dictator. The president would be elected for four years. He or she would be commander in chief of the military forces, would be primarily responsible for relations with other countries, and would ensure that the laws passed by Congress would be carried out. The president could also veto laws passed by Congress, but Congress could override that veto.

The framers thought that each branch of government would work at a different rate of speed, because each would have its own set of duties. They thought the judicial branch would act most slowly, partly because lawyers usually need time to gather

Because of his speeches, negotiations, and attempts at compromise during the Constitutional Convention, James Madison became known as the Father of the Constitution.

When Washington took the oath of office, he wondered whether he could live up to the expectations of the American people.

evidence and present their case, and because fair decisions require careful deliberation. The framers of the Constitution thought Congress would also act relatively slowly, because of the need to gather information, debate the issues, and get agreement among many members. The framers, however, wanted the president to be able to act rapidly and decisively.

When they drafted the Constitution, the framers expected that the Supreme Court would only meet at the nation's capital for a few months each year. But they intended that the president, even if he was away from the capital, would act for the nation in an emergency. The framers also wanted to be sure that in some areas—such as dealing with other nations—the United States should be as unified as

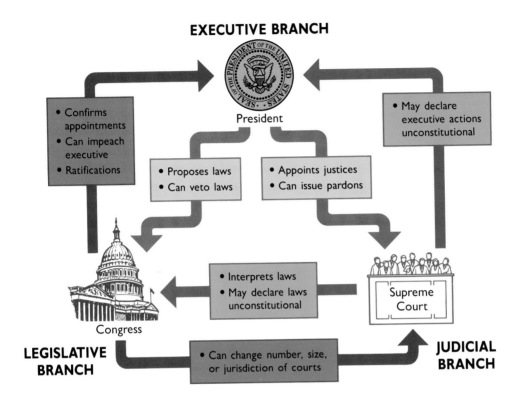

EXECUTIVE BRANCH

President

- Confirms appointments
- Can impeach executive
- Ratifications

- Proposes laws
- Can veto laws

- Appoints justices
- Can issue pardons

- May declare executive actions unconstitutional

- Interprets laws
- May declare laws unconstitutional

Congress

Supreme Court

LEGISLATIVE BRANCH

- Can change number, size, or jurisdiction of courts

JUDICIAL BRANCH

possible, and they hoped that the president would express that unity. For these reasons—speed, unity, and the ability to act in an emergency—the framers expected that the president would often be called upon to make important decisions.

This series is about the great decisions that some of our presidents have made. Of course, presidents make decisions every day. They decide whom to appoint to office, what to say to leaders of foreign nations, whether or not to veto laws passed by Congress. Most of these decisions are quite ordinary. From time to time, however, the president makes a decision that will affect the American people (and often other nations as well) for many years, maybe even centuries. You may think of Abraham Lincoln's decision to free the slaves, or Franklin Roosevelt's decision to fight the Great Depression, or John Kennedy's decision to fight for civil rights for African Americans. Of course, not every important decision our presidents have made has been wise. James Buchanan decided not to stop the Southern states from leaving the Union. Franklin Roosevelt decided to ask Congress to increase the size of the Supreme Court, so it would more often decide cases the way he wanted. Richard Nixon decided to cover up the Watergate burglary.

This book is about Ronald Reagan and the decisions he made as president. Reagan was one of the most popular presidents in American history. Although he spent many years as a movie and television actor, Reagan had natural political gifts. Besides his unusual background and his popularity, Reagan was different in important ways from most twentieth century presidents. He had a very clear philosophy. He knew less about what was happening in the government, worked less, and had less curiosity than other presidents. He also worried less when making difficult decisions.

During his eight years as president, Reagan made a number of important decisions. We will look at five of them. The last, his decision to seek arms reduction agreements with the former Soviet Union, is one of the most important decisions ever made by a president of the United States. In looking at these decisions, we will see both the strengths and the weaknesses of Ronald Reagan as president.

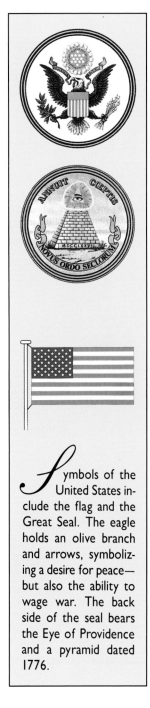

*S*ymbols of the United States include the flag and the Great Seal. The eagle holds an olive branch and arrows, symbolizing a desire for peace— but also the ability to wage war. The back side of the seal bears the Eye of Providence and a pyramid dated 1776.

The Inauguration

*J*IMMY CARTER STAYED UP ALL
night—but not just because it was his last
night as president. He was on the phone
constantly, calling about the final arrange-
ments for the release of 52 Americans held hostage
in Iran. Since the hostages had been captured 14
months earlier, Carter had worked very hard to gain
their release. His failure to do so had contributed
to his defeat for reelection by Ronald Reagan. Carter
waited at his desk, his face puffy and full of sadness.
He hoped that before he left office he could announce
the good news to the nation. Finally, Carter left the
Oval Office to shave and put on a fresh suit. The
inaugural ceremonies were about to begin.

Ronald Reagan and Jimmy Carter then got into
one limousine, Rosalynn Carter and Nancy Reagan

Chief Justice Warren Burger administered the oath of office to
69-year-old Ronald Reagan, the oldest man ever to be sworn in
as president.

President Jimmy Carter, *left,* and President-elect Ronald Reagan rode together from the White House to Reagan's inaugural ceremony at the Capitol.

into another. While they drove up Pennsylvania Avenue to the Capitol, the hostages were still being held in Iran. Besides the new president and vice president (George Bush), this inauguration introduced something else that was new. For over 150 years presidents had been sworn in on the east side of the Capitol. This time the ceremony took place on the west side. While the guests took their seats, the Marine Corps band played "Yankee Doodle" and the "Battle Hymn of the Republic." The Carters, the Reagans, and all the other high officials of the United States government were seated high on the steps of the Capitol. In front of them was a crowd of thousands. The Carters and the Reagans could see beyond the crowd to the great buildings housing the government. They could see the National Archives Building, where the Declaration of Independence and

Holding the inauguration on the west steps of the Capitol illustrated the new administration's concern with symbols and image. Traditionally inaugurations were held at the Capitiol's main entrance, on the east steps. Reagan felt the west steps turned toward the nation's development and symbolized the nation's progress. Also, Reagan was from the West, having lived in the state of California.

From the Capitol, the Reagans could see many of the great Washington buildings and monuments behind the thousands of onlookers.

the Constitution are kept. They could also see the Washington Monument and the Lincoln Memorial, built to honor two great presidential predecessors.

First, George Bush was sworn in as vice president. Then, the dignified, white-haired Warren Burger, the chief justice of the United States, rose and raised his right hand. He faced the 69-year-old Ronald Reagan, the oldest man ever to be sworn in as president. Reagan, however, looked many years younger than his age—tall, erect, and still dark-haired. Between the two men stood Nancy Reagan, holding the Bible that was used when the chief justice administered the oath of office. Then Reagan walked to the podium to give his first speech as president. At the end of his inaugural address, he spoke about Martin A. Treptow, a hero who had fought and died in World War I. In his diary Treptow had written, "America must win this war. Therefore I will work. I will sacrifice. I will endure. I will fight cheerfully and do my utmost, as if the whole struggle depended on me alone." That summed up Reagan's message to his country.

At the luncheon that followed the inauguration, the new president announced, "Some 30 minutes ago, the planes bearing our prisoners left Iranian airspace and are free of Iran." In this, as in many events of Ronald Reagan's presidency, he was able to give the American people good news.

At a luncheon following the inaugural ceremony, President Reagan announced the release of the American hostages who had been held in Iran.

Reagan's Background

*O*N FEBRUARY 6, 1911, RONALD Reagan was born in Tampico, Illinois, a little town of 800 people, located about 110 miles west of Chicago, near the Iowa border. While Reagan was a child, his family moved frequently within Illinois. They lived in Tampico, Chicago, Galesburg, Monmouth, again in Tampico, then Dixon, and Springfield. Between the ages of six and ten, Reagan went to a different school each year. Finally, the family returned to Dixon, where Reagan finished elementary school and high school.

Reagan remembers his childhood as being very happy, although there must have been many difficult moments. His father, John Edward Reagan, drank a great deal and had trouble keeping a job. Reagan's mother, Nelle, was a strong person and very religious. She loved the theater, and from her Ronald Reagan learned how much he loved to act.

Reagan's boyhood home in Dixon, Illinois.

To the right is a family portrait. From *left to right,* John, Neil, Ronald, and Nelle Reagan. *Below,* Reagan worked as a lifeguard during the summer months.

Reagan played on his high school and college football teams, took part in track and swimming meets, and appeared in many school plays. Every summer he worked as a lifeguard. Reagan was president of his high school student council and president of the student body at Eureka College in Eureka, Illinois.

After he completed college, Reagan became a sports broadcaster for a radio station in Davenport, Iowa. When the Chicago Cubs played, Reagan received little bits of information about the game over the telegraph. From that information, he invented background details to make it all sound exciting. He was very good at what he did.

A few years later, in 1937, when Reagan was in southern California to cover the Cubs' spring training, he took a screen test. Warner Brothers studio hired him. From 1937 to 1964 Reagan made more than 50 films, including westerns, war stories, romantic comedies, and sports stories. He was not a great actor, but he was a good one—excellent at memorizing lines, patient, and cooperative. Like many fine Hollywood actors of the period, Reagan was

Reagan played football at Eureka College, *above.* Following college, he became a radio sports broadcaster in Davenport, Iowa.

Ronald Reagan acted in many movies, such as *Bedtime for Bonzo, right,* and *Law and Order, below.*

best at playing the part of a good, honest, trusting, laid-back kind of guy—the sort of person he was in real life. He played the Notre Dame halfback, George Gipp, in *Knute Rockne: All American;* the baseball pitcher Grover Cleveland Alexander in *The Winning Team;* and opposite a chimpanzee in *Bedtime for Bonzo.*

Reagan met actress Jane Wyman while they were both appearing in Warner Brothers films. The couple was married January 25, 1940. During World War II, Reagan served in the First Motion Picture Unit of the Army Air Corps. While he was in the army, Jane gave birth to a daughter, Maureen Elizabeth. Fortunately, Reagan was able to commute

Reagan and his first wife, movie star Jane Wyman, hold their nine-month-old daughter, Maureen Elizabeth.

from his base to his nearby home on weekends. The couple also adopted a son, Michael Edward, in 1945. In 1948, the marriage ended in divorce. A few years later, Reagan met and married Nancy Davis. With Nancy, Reagan also had two children, a daughter, Patricia Ann, and a son, Ronald Prescott.

During this period, Reagan was very active in the Screen Actors Guild (SAG), an actors' union. He served five consecutive terms as president of the Guild from 1947 to 1952. During that time, which was a period of strong anti-Communist feeling in the United States, Reagan fought the perceived

On March 4, 1952, Reagan married another movie star, Nancy Davis, *right*.

Communist influence in the union and in the movie industry. Serving a sixth term as SAG president (from 1959 to 1960), Reagan led a successful strike against the movie industry to win payments for actors from the sale of their old films to television.

From 1954 to 1962, Reagan hosted the *General Electric Theater,* a weekly dramatic series on television. When his involvement with that show ended, Reagan hosted and performed in a western series called *Death Valley Days.*

In the meantime, Reagan had taken an active interest in politics. At first he held liberal views and belonged to the Democratic Party. President Franklin Roosevelt was his great hero, and he campaigned for President Harry Truman in 1948. During the 1950s, however, his views became more conservative. This may be due in part to his marriage to Nancy, who came from a very conservative family. Reagan campaigned for Dwight Eisenhower, the Republican candidate for president in 1952 and 1956, and for Richard Nixon in 1960, but he did not register as a Republican until 1962. While hosting the *General Electric Theater,* Reagan acted as a public relations representative for General Electric, the sponsor of the program. He traveled throughout the United States for General Electric, making speeches about the importance of the free enterprise system and the dangers of too much federal control. He spoke at General Electric plants, chambers of commerce, and various civic organizations. Sometimes he gave as many as 14 speeches a day. Before he finished, Reagan had traveled to 38 states and spoken to approximately 250,000 General Electric employees.

A young Ronald Reagan testified at a House Committee on UnAmerican Activities (HUAC) hearing in 1947. He fought against any perceived Communist influence in the movie industry.

In 1966 Reagan ran for governor of California, *below.* In 1968 he campaigned for presidential candidate Richard Nixon, *right.*

Ronald Reagan first gained nationwide political attention when he gave a televised speech on behalf of Republican presidential nominee Barry Goldwater in 1964. In the speech Reagan attacked high taxes, wasteful government spending, rising crime rates, and soaring welfare costs.

In 1966 Reagan ran for governor of California, then the nation's second-largest state. He won 57.6 percent of the vote against the state's incumbent Democratic governor, Edmund G. ("Pat") Brown. Four years later, Reagan easily won reelection. As governor of California, Reagan slowed the growth of spending by the state government. Although he sponsored three tax increases, once the state budget showed a surplus, he returned much of the excess to the taxpayers.

Governor Ronald Reagan

Reagan tried to become the Republican candidate for president in 1968, but lost to Richard Nixon. He tried again in 1976, but lost to President Gerald Ford by a narrow margin. At the age of 69, Reagan tried again in 1980. Winning 20 of 24 primaries, he easily became the Republican nominee, and chose as his running mate one of the candidates he had defeated, George Bush.

Through most of September and October 1980, the presidential race between Reagan and incumbent president Jimmy Carter appeared to be very close, but in the election Reagan won by a wide margin. He received 44 million popular votes to Carter's 35 million. Carter won only 6 states and the District of Columbia—with a total of 49 electoral votes. Reagan captured 44 states, with 489 electoral votes.

CHAPTER THREE

Reagan's Qualifications

*M*ANY LAWYERS, A NUMBER OF generals, a couple of engineers, and a journalist have become president of the United States. Ronald Reagan, however, was the first professional actor to become president, and some people thought, because of that, he wasn't qualified. While it is true that he had many limitations, Reagan had been governor of California for eight years. He also had considerable political experience and a number of talents that suited him extremely well for the presidency—at least as he saw the president's role.

Beyond this, Reagan had some remarkable abilities and personality traits. He was a secure and self-confident man, who would almost never be troubled by the great pressures of the presidency.

A very popular president, Reagan addressed the crowd at the 1984 Republican convention. Delegates enthusiastically nominated him for a second term.

Reagan was able to transfer his optimism to a wide sector of the American public.

He was optimistic—and remained so even after he was shot, the *Challenger* space shuttle blew up, and a summit meeting broke up in apparent failure. Reagan liked people and people liked him. He was a genuinely good-natured man, who never bore grudges. Although his political beliefs seemed extreme to some Americans, he never treated (or thought of) those Americans who opposed him as enemies. His natural warmth made him able to establish exceptionally close relations with several leaders of other countries. Reagan's political sense was brilliant. He seemed to know by instinct what Americans cared about most.

An attempted assassination of Reagan occurred in Washington, D.C., in March 1981, *above*. He was shot in the chest, but surgeons removed the bullet, and he recovered. His wife, Nancy, visits him in the hospital, *left*.

President Reagan was popular among foreign heads of state. Here, he chats with Margaret Thatcher, who was then prime minister of England.

His experience and talent as an actor were essential to the type of president he wanted to be. He communicated to the American people that he shared their hopes and fears, that he could lead the country, that his policies were wise, and that the future was golden. Reagan soothed most people's fears. The American people saw him as an old and trustworthy friend.

Reagan also had serious weaknesses. He didn't have the knowledge of history, government, or politics that John Kennedy, Lyndon Johnson, or Richard Nixon had. He often confused fact and fiction. He lacked intellectual curiosity. He did not like to work hard. His energy level declined after he was shot in an attempted assassination in 1981, and it declined further with age. He was 77 years old when he left office. In Reagan's first term, most Americans seemed to see only his strong traits. In his second term, they saw many of his weak ones.

The Situation When Reagan Became President

*W*HEN RONALD REAGAN BECAME president in 1981, the American people seemed to have lost confidence in America. In less than 20 years, the United States had lived through the assassinations of President John Kennedy, presidential candidate Robert Kennedy, civil rights leader Martin Luther King, Jr., and the attempted assassinations of President Gerald Ford and presidential candidate George Wallace. Serious racial unrest threatened the country in the 1960s. America's racial problems were still far from solved. For the first time in its history, the United States had lost a war (in Vietnam)—a war that had bitterly divided

Huge crowds were on hand in the streets of Tehran, Iran, to welcome Shiite Muslim leader Ayatollah Khomeini when he returned from exile. He is the bearded man waving to the crowd.

Two Soviet tanks set up positions outside the city of Kabul, Afghanistan, in January 1980.

the American people. Also for the first time, a president of the United States, Richard Nixon, had resigned in disgrace to avoid impeachment. Nixon was accused of a variety of crimes, as were his vice president, Spiro T. Agnew, and a number of his closest assistants. The American economy, for so long the strongest in the world, had begun to weaken. Due to inflation, prices rose at the rate of 13 percent a year. Nations in the Middle East began to sell less oil, causing long lines at gas stations. Gasoline and oil became very expensive. At the same time, the number of unemployed workers had begun to grow, and the U.S. economy was falling behind those of West Germany and Japan.

Iranian students demonstrated in front of the American embassy, where they were holding 52 people hostage, *left*. The scarecrow represents Uncle Sam. The deposed Shah Mohammad Reza Pahlavi is above.

Many people thought that U.S. military strength had fallen behind that of the Soviet Union in the late 1970s. The Cold War was still going on, and at the end of 1979, the Soviet Union invaded Afghanistan and seemed to be successfully challenging the influence of the United States in Africa and Central America. Terrorist groups from the Middle East were

On the first day of gas
rationing, dozens of cars
lined up at this station in
Los Angeles, California.

kidnapping Americans and hijacking American commercial airplanes, and the United States did not seem to be able to do anything about it. By 1980 the American people felt frustrated and discouraged. That discouragement and frustration came to a head during the Iranian hostage crisis.

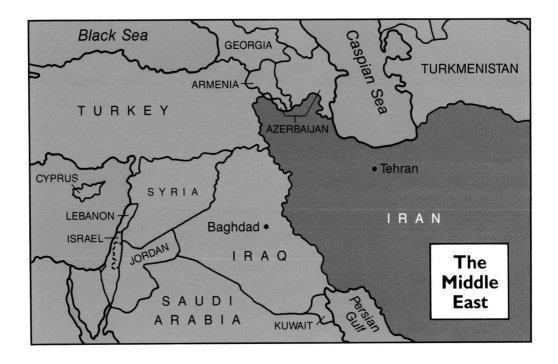

Early in 1979, Shah Mohammad Reza Pahlavi, the leader of Iran, fled his country in the midst of a revolution brought about by traditional Shiite Muslim groups. The shah had long been a friend to the United States, and Iran had been a powerful and important U.S. ally in the Middle East. A revolutionary Islamic republic led by an aged and fanatical religious leader, the Ayatollah Ruhollah Khomeini, replaced the shah's government. In October 1979, President Jimmy Carter allowed the deposed shah to enter the United States for medical treatment. In protest, hundreds of Iranian revolutionaries stormed the U.S. embassy in Tehran, the capital of Iran, on November 4, 1979. They captured 66 Americans, holding 52 of them hostage. They demanded that the United States return the

Middle East

*A*t the time Ronald Reagan became president, the Middle East (the area close to the Mediterranean Sea from Iran in the east to Morocco in the west and from Iraq and Turkey in the north to the Sudan in the south) had been causing major problems for the United States for over 30 years. The United States had three important interests in the Middle East: keeping the Soviet Union out of the area; helping the state of Israel to survive; and producing oil. Middle Eastern nations such as Iran, Iraq, Saudi Arabia, and Kuwait are important suppliers of oil to the United States. Since the creation of Israel from part of Palestine in 1948 as a homeland for the Jewish people, the United States has supported Israel. This support for Israel caused friction with other nations in the area. One of the only democracies in an area where cruel dictators were often in power, Israel was also the strongest military power in the area, surviving wars fought against it by most of its neighbors in 1945, 1956, 1967, and 1973.

Jimmy Carter, who was president before Ronald Reagan, had helped to bring peace between Israel and one of its strongest enemies, Egypt. At the time Ronald Reagan became president, however, the Palestine Liberation Organization (PLO), which aimed to create a homeland for the Palestinian people, seemed to be gaining strength.

In addition, when Reagan became president, Lebanon, one of the few democracies in the region other than Israel, was in the midst of a raging civil war in which its neighbors, Syria and Israel, had become involved. The United States had also lost the support of Iran, an important ally, when the ruling shah was overthrown. A revolutionary Islamic regime strongly opposed to the United States replaced the shah's government.

shah to Iran for trial in exchange for the hostages, but President Carter refused. In April 1980, he authorized an armed rescue mission to free the hostages, but it failed. In July the shah died in Egypt, but the Iranian revolutionaries continued to hold the hostages until January 20, 1981, the day Carter left office.

During his presidency, Carter had come to represent the nation's loss of confidence. He had told the American people in 1979 that the nation was in a crisis that "strikes at the very heart and soul and spirit of our national will." He said, "For the first time in the history of our country, a majority of our people believe that the next five years will be worse than the past five years." Carter was held responsible for the weak economy, for the long lines at the gas pumps, for being unable to stop the invasion of Afghanistan, for not being able to stop the decline of respect for the United States, and especially responsible for failing to secure the release of the hostages.

Since the assassination of John F. Kennedy in 1963, the United States had had a series of presidents—Johnson, Nixon, Ford, and Carter—who had each lost the confidence of the people. Ronald Reagan tried to help the American people regain their confidence in the presidency and in the United States.

As president, Jimmy Carter was determined to free the American hostages in Iran, but he failed to do so before he left office.

Reagan's Principles

ONALD REAGAN BELIEVED IN A set of principles that provided him with much of the agenda he wanted to carry out as president. First, he wanted to reduce the size of the U.S. government and the amount of government spending. The people, Reagan thought, believed that "government isn't the answer." Reagan thought that many things government was doing could be done better by private enterprise. He believed that having too many government programs caused an increase in taxes and that taxes were consuming too much of the nation's wealth. He thought lower taxes would make the United States a more productive country, because money would then be available for investment. Reagan also believed that some

President Reagan delivered his 1984 State of the Union address to Congress on January 25. He had been very successful in getting his programs through Congress during his first term in office.

As president, Reagan enjoyed attending public ceremonies, such as the 100th birthday celebration of the Statue of Liberty, *right,* and reviewing the troops at the recommissioning of the U.S.S. *New Jersey, below.*

fundamental American freedoms were endangered by government bureaucrats who had too much control over businesses, dictated to state and city governments, and made decisions the people should make for themselves.

Reagan hated Communism. He viewed the Soviet Union as the center of "an evil empire." He believed that in order to ensure peace, the United States had to spend much more money on arms. But he was also convinced that the huge number of nuclear weapons the United States and the Soviet Union had aimed at each other were "horrible missiles of destruction" that could, within minutes, "destroy virtually the civilized world we live in."

Most of all, Ronald Reagan believed in America. He worried that America was losing faith in itself. He saw Americans as "God's chosen people," their country as "the promised land," and their government as "the last best hope on earth."

Reagan's Presidential Style

RONALD REAGAN'S DISTINCTIVE style as president was that of performer. What he liked most about the presidency (and did so well) was its public side—making speeches and attending ceremonies. He used such appearances not only to build support for his programs and for himself, but also to build confidence in the presidency and in America.

With the aid of some fine speechwriters (though Reagan himself rewrote his speeches more often than most recent presidents), Reagan gave some eloquent and moving speeches. For example, in a television address the evening after the space shuttle *Challenger* blew up, Reagan spoke to the nation. In part of his speech, he spoke directly to the families of the crew. "Your loved ones," he said, "were daring

With a crowd of supporters on hand, the president and Mrs. Reagan leave the White House en route to Camp David for the weekend during March 1987.

and brave and they had that special grace, that special spirit that says, 'Give me a challenge and I'll meet it with joy.'" In that speech, he also spoke to the nation's schoolchildren, many of whom had watched the take-off and seen the explosion on television. He said, "I know it's hard to understand, but sometimes painful things like this happen—it's all part of taking a chance and expanding man's horizons. The future doesn't belong to the fainthearted, it belongs to the brave. The *Challenger* crew was pulling us into the future—and we'll continue to follow them."

On the 40th anniversary of the D day landings by the United States and its allies on the coast of France during World War II, Reagan gave a speech at the windswept cliffs of Pointe du Hoc, France. There, on June 6, 1944, a group of U.S. Rangers had overcome enormous German resistance and climbed a 100-foot cliff to gain a critical foothold in France and begin the final defeat of the Nazis. This is part of what Reagan said:

Ronald Reagan as George Gipp in the movie *Knute Rockne: All-American*

> Forty years ago as I speak they were fighting to hold these cliffs. They had radioed back and asked for reinforcements and they were told: There aren't any. But they did not give up. It was not in them to give up. They would not be turned back; they held the cliffs.
>
> Two hundred twenty-five came here. After a day of fighting, only ninety could still bear arms.

Then, Reagan turned to many of the surviving Rangers, now middle-aged to elderly, sitting in the audience. He said, "These are the boys of Pointe du Hoc. These are the men who took the cliffs. These

From the White House, President Reagan comforted the nation when the space shuttle *Challenger* exploded in midair above Cape Canaveral, Florida.

are the champions who helped free a continent. These are the heroes who helped end a war."

Reagan was using his speeches to help rebuild the confidence of Americans in America. He believed deeply in America as a special land with a special history and destiny, as a "land of the free" that delivers on its promises for "most of the people most of the time." He used great spectacles to dramatize his love for his country and his confidence in it. At the 1984 Olympic Games in Los Angeles, surrounded by a crowd waving American flags, he called on U.S. athletes to "Win one for the Gipper," referring to a movie role he had once played. In New York Harbor in 1986, on the 100th birthday of the Statue of Liberty, Reagan pushed a button that sent a laser beam out to light the torch. In his

The Reagans attended the 1984 Olympic Games in Los Angeles, California, *right*. At the 40th anniversary of the D-day landings during World War II, the president gave a speech at Pointe du Hoc, France, where the Allies had landed in 1944.

speech, he once again reminded Americans of their special freedoms. By and large, Reagan was remarkably successful in transferring his great confidence in America to the American people, who were hungry for good news and leadership.

He was less enthusiastic about and less talented at thinking through policies and seeing that they were being carried out by members of his administration. Because he often made factual errors or seemed confused when talking with the press, Reagan's chief aides planned his presidency as if Reagan were still an actor. Every word was scripted, every moment planned. Every place he stood in ceremonies was marked with chalk. Rather than giving directions to his administration as a film director or a film producer might, Reagan, as president, was for most of the time an actor who followed directions. The presidency, however, requires more than just reciting prepared lines. A president must lead, and a president must decide.

Reagan as a Decision Maker

*R*ONALD REAGAN WAS DIFFERENT from almost all our presidents because he was a superb performer and because he came to office with a clear set of principles to guide him. He was also different in that he knew less about the policies of his administration and was less interested in the day-to-day details of governing than any modern president. On the other hand, Reagan knew what direction he wanted the United States to go, kept focused on the four or five goals he really cared about, and agonized less in making difficult decisions than any recent president.

Reagan came to office knowing that he wanted lower taxes, a smaller federal government, more money spent on defense, tough negotiations with the Soviet Union, an end to the nuclear arms race, and America's confidence in itself restored. He

Jim Baker, the White House chief of staff during Reagan's first term, meets with the president in the Oval Office.

never changed his mind about any of these goals. He kept trying to accomplish them and remained optimistic about achieving them, even when, as with an end to the nuclear arms race, they seemed impossible to attain. He focused on these goals and spent relatively little time on others.

One of Reagan's greatest strengths was his ability to make tough decisions quickly and, once they were made, to stick with them without further worry. Reagan did not actively seek information about the decisions he had to make. This meant his chief advisers had to think through problems carefully and present the president with clear choices before he could make an informed decision. Once that happened, Reagan did not agonize over decisions the way most recent presidents have. His first secretary of state, Alexander Haig, called him "the most graceful and easy decision maker I've ever seen." Once Reagan made a decision, he was masterful at communicating it to the nation.

Although Reagan felt strongly about the principles he believed in, he also knew when to compromise. While on some matters—such as more money for national defense—Reagan was unyielding, on others he knew when to settle for a little less. He was also able to fight political battles without making personal attacks on other politicians. Indeed, he got along well with almost all of his political opponents.

Those were Reagan's great strengths in making decisions. He also had great weaknesses. He did not work hard. He lacked factual knowledge of some issues and rarely made an effort to inform himself. He organized the White House in such a way that

Reagan relaxes at his ranch near Santa Barbara, California.

he had to rely almost completely on his advisers for information. Most of the time he was not interested in how policy was carried out, which left him vulnerable if his aides abused their authority.

Reagan was completely unlike Lyndon Johnson and Richard Nixon, both of whom felt the need to work almost constantly. Reagan needed rest and relaxation. Although he was in good physical condition for his age, he was, nevertheless, almost 70 years old when he became president. When he was wounded in an assassination attempt, it took him a long time—much longer than the White House initially admitted—to fully regain his energy.

While Johnson and Nixon worked 12-to-16-hour days, Reagan worked from 9:00 A.M. to 5:30 P.M. five days a week, often taking Wednesday afternoons off. Many weekends he helicoptered to Camp David, the presidential retreat in Maryland. Reagan also spent over 10 percent of his presidency (345 days out of 2,762) on his ranch—vacationing much of the time. Reagan's first adviser for national security, Richard Allen, explained this pace with some wit: "He was a highly intelligent man who, when confronted with big workloads and easy workloads, would always pick the easy workloads." When on the job, Reagan devoted much of his energy to speeches and ceremonies.

Keeping to an orderly schedule and pacing oneself can lead to a better presidency for workaholic presidents, who often get caught up in little details and then make important decisions within an exhausted frame of mind. But Reagan needed to work much harder than he did, because there was so much that he just didn't know. For example, he did not know

Both Lyndon B. Johnson, *top,* and Richard M. Nixon, *bottom,* were "workaholic" presidents, in sharp contrast to Ronald Reagan.

that the Soviet strategic force was heavily concentrated on land-based missiles. He did not know that as a result of his administration's policy, there had been cutbacks in education. His grasp of names was especially bad. Once, when talking with House Speaker "Tip" O'Neill, Reagan even confused Grover Cleveland, the former president, with Grover Cleveland Alexander, the baseball pitcher he had once played in a motion picture.

This lack of knowledge might not have been so serious if Reagan had worked to overcome it, but he didn't. He preferred watching movies and television or reading adventure novels to reading briefing

The Reagans enjoy horseback riding at their ranch.

The president spent many weekends at Camp David. Here, he meets with Richard Allen, Reagan's first national security adviser.

books that would have provided him with important information. Indeed, his advisers often had to use films, cartoons, multiple choice tests, and anecdotes to brief him. When he met with congressmen, cabinet officials, and other American leaders, Reagan usually relied on three-by-five index cards for his comments. Once when he was meeting with the heads of the largest U.S. automobile companies to talk about trade with other nations, Reagan began the discussion with remarks that had nothing to do with any subject relevant to that meeting. It turned out he had taken the wrong set of index cards to the meeting. Republican leaders in Congress tried several times to talk with Reagan about arms control. They found he listened to them, but only responded by reading his index cards. Eventually they gave up and talked with his advisers.

For making decisions, modern presidents have usually tried to organize the White House in one of two very different ways. One way is especially

Reagan as baseball pitcher Grover Cleveland Alexander in *The Winning Team,* 1952

President Reagan with his cabinet and Vice President George Bush, *right*. The president watches a football game, *below*.

organized and orderly, but the president is less accessible. President Dwight Eisenhower, who had been a great general, used a model based on military organization. He delegated many decisions to members of his cabinet. Communications to the president—letters, memos, even phone calls—went through channels to the White House chief of staff. When President Eisenhower had to make decisions, he often called his cabinet or National Security Council together. They had a set agenda. The president listened to discussion at the meeting and then made his decision.

The other method of organization, that used by Franklin D. Roosevelt, is much less orderly, but it allows the president greater information and greater access to differing opinions. Formal meetings and chains of command were much less important in

As president, Reagan often relied on prepared index cards for information.

Dwight D. Eisenhower

Franklin D. Roosevelt

Roosevelt's White House. The president himself saw a very wide variety of advisers including cabinet members, professors, and labor and business leaders. He was the moving force in his presidency. He was the hub of the wheel; his many advisers, the spokes. The process was disorderly. Aides and cabinet members attacked one another in memos, in the press, and sometimes in front of the president. Sometimes the president gave responsibility to deal with the same problem to officials from different parts of the government. This system worked for Roosevelt, because he was ever curious and energetic.

Ronald Reagan's approach was much closer to that of President Eisenhower's. In his first term, Reagan had three aides who could see him at any time and who controlled the flow of information to him: Jim Baker (who was the White House chief of staff), Mike Deaver (who controlled the president's schedule), and Ed Meese (who served as legal counsel to the president and whose political principles were the closest to Reagan's). These three men knew Reagan's strengths and his limitations. Where he was weak, they could help him. This was particularly important because Reagan was not a curious or energetic president like Roosevelt. He rarely called a meeting, asked for a progress report, or tried to get information on his own. Reagan seldom even made a telephone call without one of his three advisers suggesting it. He was a passive president, who believed that he hired people he trusted, and he would let them do the job. David Stockman, his budget director during his first term, said, "He gave no orders, no commands, asked for no information, expressed no urgency."

Sometimes the general policy directions Reagan gave could be easily carried out. At other times, however, officials in his government were bitterly divided over what should be done. Meetings in which they explained their disagreements could have taught Reagan about the risks of different policies,

Jim Baker, *standing left*, and Donald Regan, *standing right*, joke with President Reagan in the Oval Office.

as they did Roosevelt. But this remarkably good-natured man hated conflict in his presence. At meetings where there were distressing arguments, he would withdraw from the conflict and not take sides. His advisers often left meetings unsure as to what Reagan wanted or how he wanted it carried out. Advisers who disagreed as strongly as Secretary of State George Schultz and Secretary of Defense Caspar Weinberger continued their fights by leaks to the press. Ronald Reagan's approach to decision making sometimes left much to be desired, but it also produced a number of major successes.

Secretary of State George Schultz, *front left,* and Secretary of Defense Caspar Weinberger, *front right,* frequently disagreed with each other.

The Decision to Cut Taxes and Increase Defense Spending

*P*ERHAPS THE MOST IMPORTANT decision made by President Reagan during his first term was to concentrate on fighting for just two goals: reducing taxes and raising defense spending. By doing this and also cutting some government spending programs, the Reagan administration got off to a good start. The president earned a reputation for political savvy from these early victories. The fight for the tax cut and higher defense spending showed Reagan's flexibility and talent as a communicator, but it also showed the lack of knowledge Reagan and most of his advisers had about important economic facts.

As head of the Office of Management and Budget, David Stockman, *standing front,* encouraged President Reagan to cut taxes, decrease spending for government programs, and increase defense spending.

From left to right, presidential aides James Baker (White House chief of staff), Edward Meese (legal counsel to the president), and Michael Deaver (who controlled the president's schedule)

When Reagan became president, he had not decided what his priorities would be in translating his principles into action. His aides—Baker, Deaver, and Meese—had not thought much about it either. However, David Stockman, the new 34-year-old head of the Office of Management and Budget, had thought about it. Stockman convinced Reagan and his advisers to concentrate on taxes, defense spending, and making cuts in government programs. Stockman believed that Congress had to be pushed quickly, before opponents of the policies could get organized. He thought that if Congress acted immediately, the economy would improve rapidly, and it would then be difficult to reverse what had been done.

Because the administration wanted to move quickly, Reagan's advisers had little time to master the federal budget, an enormously complicated subject. On February 18, 1981, less than a month after he took office, Ronald Reagan addressed the Congress. He called for cutting taxes by 30 percent, increasing defense spending by three-fourths of a trillion dollars, and making reductions in 83 federal programs. This program would, he said, lead to a balanced budget within three years.

President Reagan was a superb lobbyist for his program. Less than 30 days after he was shot, Reagan again went before Congress to speak on behalf of his program. His aides in the White House showed how well they had mastered congressional budget procedures. The Senate passed the Economic Recovery Act of 1981 by a vote of 89 to 11, and the House of Representatives passed the bill by a vote of 239 to 195. The law lowered individual income taxes and corporate income taxes by 33 billion dollars for the 1982 fiscal year (September 1, 1982 to August 31, 1983) with more cuts scheduled for later. This was the largest income tax cut in U.S. history. When the bill for national defense passed, the Reagan administration achieved the largest peacetime defense buildup in American history.

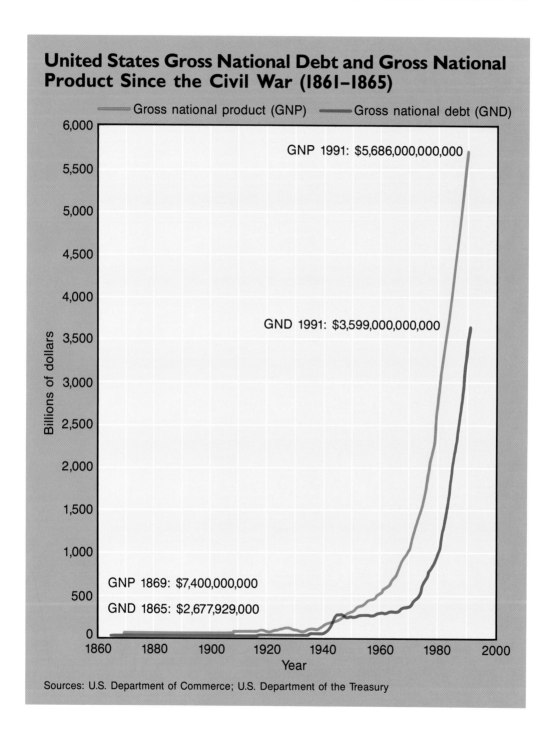

United States Gross National Debt and Gross National Product Since the Civil War (1861–1865)

Gross national product (GNP)   Gross national debt (GND)

GNP 1991: $5,686,000,000,000

GND 1991: $3,599,000,000,000

GNP 1869: $7,400,000,000

GND 1865: $2,677,929,000

Billions of dollars

Year

Sources: U.S. Department of Commerce; U.S. Department of the Treasury

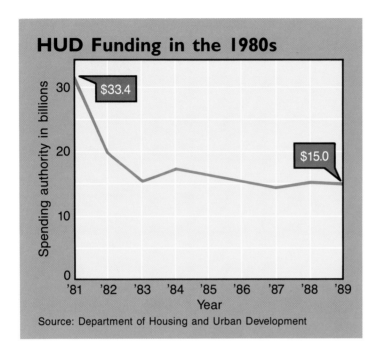

HUD Funding in the 1980s

Source: Department of Housing and Urban Development

Budget cuts for low-income housing and federal assistance programs for the poor contributed to an increase in homelessness in the 1980s.

But Stockman did not tell Reagan and his aides that unless there were extraordinarily deep reductions in federal programs, the United States would increase its debt by an enormous amount every year. As spending increased year by year, money taken in by taxes decreased. Reagan and his aides misjudged the willingness of members of Congress to make big cuts in federal programs, such as social security and veterans benefits, that many of their constituents strongly supported. Indeed, even the Reagan appointees who headed executive departments, such as Health and Human Services, the Department of Energy, and the Justice Department, did not want their programs cut. Nevertheless, several major programs did get cut. Government welfare programs were sharply reduced—programs such as rent subsidies for the poor, school lunch subsidies, and job training. Other programs, including Medicare health insurance and Head Start preschool education, were continued—but this "safety net" was not nearly enough to meet even the basic needs of the very poor.

Margaret Heckler, Secretary of the Department of Health and Human Services under Ronald Reagan

Ronald Reagan's economic program produced the largest budget deficit in American history. Reagan, a man who deeply believed in a small federal government and a balanced budget, ended up raising the national debt more than all of the presidents before him combined.

This result did not greatly distress Ronald Reagan. Cutting taxes and increasing defense spending were more important to him than balancing the budget. Having such a large deficit also made it very difficult to increase the size of the federal government with any new nondefense spending programs, and

Reagan's economic plan included a large increase in defense spending.

What We Got for $2 Trillion
Pentagon spending increases 65% during the Reagan years

Branch	Item	1980	1988	Change
Army	Personnel	776,000	772,000	− 4,000
	Tanks	10,985	16,316	+ 5,331
Air Force	Fighter, attack aircraft (includes reserves)	2,472	2,544	+ 72
	Bombers	376	275	− 101
	Interceptors	384	258	− 126
	Airlift aircraft	890	873	− 17
Navy	Nuclear submarines	36	35	− 1
	Cruisers, destroyers, frigates	180	221	+ 41
	Carriers	12	14	+ 2
	Battleships	0	4	+ 4
	Attack submarines	82	100	+ 18
Strategic Nuclear Launchers	ICBMs	1,052	1,000	− 52
	Submarine-launched ballistic missiles	576	624	+ 48
	Bombers	316	360	+ 44
Total Nuclear Warheads		9,566	12,978	+ 3,412

Note: Figures represent U.S. forces in place at end of 1980 and 1988. Latest Air Force figures represent forces projected in fiscal 1990 Defense Dept. budget.
USN&WR—Basic data: Center for Defense Information, Congressional Research Service, U.S. Dept. of Defense, International Institute for Strategic studies

Taxes and Spending

*G*overnments have always needed to tax in order to raise money for the cost of the government and for government programs. Governments spend money for such things as building highways and bridges, education, and defense. In the United States, the principal tax—which pays for the cost of the U.S. government—is the income tax, a tax on the money a person makes each year. However, many of those who live in the United States also pay income taxes to the state they live in, as well as other taxes such as that on goods bought in stores (sales tax), and special taxes on gasoline and on cigarettes.

A deficit in government spending occurs when the amount of taxes coming in one year is less than the amount of money the government pays out. The higher a deficit is, the more money the government must pay for interest on the money it needs to borrow to pay for the deficit. A large deficit may also contribute to inflation (sharply rising prices). Small government deficits, however, may help the economy because they increase the amount of money spent, which helps to create jobs.

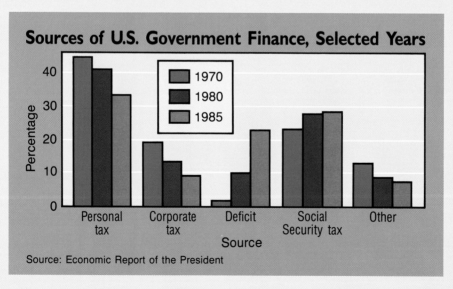

Sources of U.S. Government Finance, Selected Years

Source: Economic Report of the President

On February 18, 1981, Reagan called on Congress to cut taxes by 30 percent.

Reagan was happy with that result. The Reagan policies were very successful from 1981 to 1986. Thirteen million new jobs were created, though few of these went to unskilled workers. The stock market boomed. Inflation dropped dramatically. Real family income increased. However, the boom came to an end in 1986. Cuts in government spending hurt the poorest segment of society while the wealthiest segment increased their gains. The large deficit that began with Reagan remains a serious problem for the country. It means that much government spending must go to pay interest on the debt. Unless taxes rise, that money is unavailable to pay for national needs—an end result that satisfies the conservative goal to defer programs that enlarge the national government.

CHAPTER NINE

The Decision to Send Marines to Lebanon

*L*EBANON, A COUNTRY SMALLER than Connecticut, is located at the eastern end of the Mediterranean Sea. Israel lies to its south and Syria to its east and north. Until the 1970s, Lebanon was a center for trade and banking, a stable and relatively wealthy country. In 1975, however, a bloody civil war began, which involved various Christian and Muslim groups. The situation was further complicated by the presence of the Palestine Liberation Organization (PLO), a group whose goal was to establish a Palestinian state.

In 1981 Syria sent thousands of troops into Lebanon, and in 1982 Israeli troops, concerned about

In 1982 President Reagan decided to send a small force of U.S. Marines to Lebanon on a peacekeeping mission, but the situation soon escalated.

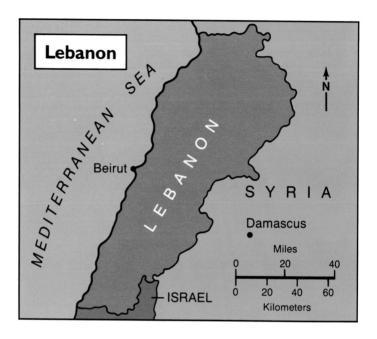

attacks on Israel by PLO forces based in southern Lebanon, invaded the country. There was not much opposition in southern Lebanon, and Israeli troops advanced very rapidly through half the country, reaching the capital city of Beirut, where many PLO leaders and troops—as well as Palestinian refugees—were living. The Soviet Union provided support for Syria; the United States for Israel. Fighting in and around Beirut was bloody, and many civilians were killed. By 1982, 100,000 people had been killed in Lebanon out of a total population of less than 3,000,000.

Reagan sent a diplomat, Philip Habib, to try to bring an end to the bloodshed. Habib was able to negotiate a truce so that the Palestinian soldiers could be evacuated from Lebanon to Tunisia, a small country in North Africa. To reach an agree-

Philip Habib, *center,* was able to negotiate a truce in Lebanon to evacuate Palestinian soldiers. Here he meets with President Reagan, *left,* and Secretary of State George Schultz, *right.*

ment, Habib had to promise that the United States, along with other countries, would send a small number of troops to Beirut. Reagan agreed to this in a phone conversation.

On August 25, 1982, 800 U.S. Marines landed in Lebanon. The marines joined forces from France and Italy to supervise the peaceful evacuation of the PLO troops. They were wedged in between 30,000 Israeli troops and 15,000 Syrian and Palestinian soldiers.

When the U.S. Marines were ordered back to their ships on September 10, their mission appeared to have been successful. All the PLO troops had been evacuated. The Syrian troops had left West Beirut, as they had promised. The Christian leader Bashir Gemayel had been elected the new president of Lebanon, and it looked as though the civil war might end.

Then, on September 14, nine days before he was to take office, president-elect Bashir Gemayel was assassinated. In response, Israeli troops reentered West Beirut, violating the agreement under which the PLO

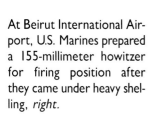

At Beirut International Airport, U.S. Marines prepared a 155-millimeter howitzer for firing position after they came under heavy shelling, *right*.

had been evacuated. Christian militiamen massacred hundreds of Palestinian refugees, without intervention from the Israelis.

In response, Reagan decided to send the marines back to Lebanon—against the advice of the Joint Chiefs of Staff. The goal, Reagan announced in a televised speech, was now to restore "a strong and central government" in Lebanon. The multinational force "is not to act as a police force, but to make it possible for the lawful authorities of Lebanon to discharge those duties for themselves." As Reagan later put it: "The purpose of having our troops and those of the other three nations in Beirut was to help keep the peace and to free the Lebanese army to go after the various militias and warlords who were terrorizing the country."

But the U.S. ability to influence events in Lebanon lessened. The Lebanese parliament unanimously elected Amin Gemayel, Bashir's brother, as president, but the government was very weak. Tension and conflict persisted, and the Soviet Union sent missiles to rearm Syria. Shiite Muslims in Lebanon tried to gain political power. They also began to believe that the U.S. troops were not neutral, but rather were there to save Lebanon's Christian-dominated government that the Muslims didn't want. Violence occurred in Lebanon again on April 18, 1983, when a delivery van full of explosives blew up on the grounds of the U.S. embassy in Beirut. Tragically, 63 people were killed, including 17 Americans.

By September 1983, the Lebanese government, rather than becoming stronger as had been hoped, actually had become weaker. Instead of remaining neutral, or withdrawing as the Israelis had done, U.S. forces began to support the Lebanese army. For the first time, artillery from U.S. destroyers and air strikes attacked the strongholds of Muslim groups. Many Muslims viewed the marines as a military prop for the minority Christian government rather than as peacekeepers.

President-elect Bashir Gemayel was killed when a bomb hit his headquarters in East Beirut.

On October 23, at 6:22 in the morning, a young man with a bushy mustache drove a yellow Mercedes truck into the parking lot of the four-story building where the marines of the First Batallion of the Eighth Regiment were sleeping. The truck driver drove over a barbed wire obstacle, passed between two marine guard posts, entered an open gate, flattened a sandbagged booth at the building's entrance, entered the lobby of the building, and blew up the truck. The explosion ripped the building from its foundation and caused it to collapse upon itself. Two hundred forty-one marines died. Reagan called it "the saddest day of my presidency—perhaps, the saddest day of my life."

Reagan now had to decide whether to send large numbers of troops to Lebanon or withdraw from the country. Congress was deeply concerned. Public opinion—as well as Reagan's military advisers and his secretary of defense—favored withdrawal. On February 5, 1984, the Gemayel government collapsed. Finally, on February 7, 1984, three and a half months after the terrorist attack on the marines, Reagan decided to withdraw the troops. The marines returned to their ships, off the coast of Lebanon. The marines were finally out of Lebanon. Another president, convinced that Lebanon was vital to U.S. interests, concerned with national honor, or afraid to appear weak, might have decided to send more troops. Reagan, however, was wise enough to know when to go. With rare candor for an American president, he admitted his mistake in his autobiography:

Through the rubble, rescue workers carried the body of a victim of the bomb blast at the U.S. embassy on April 18, 1983.

We had to pull out. By then, there was no question about it: Our policy wasn't working. We couldn't stay there and run the risk of another suicide attack on the marines. No one wanted to commit our troops to a full-scale war in the Middle East. But we couldn't remain in Lebanon and be in the war on a halfway basis, leaving our men vulnerable to terrorists with one hand tied behind their backs.

Three U.S. Marine M-60 tanks crossed the beach to navy landing craft as the marines withdrew from Beirut. The skyline of the city is in the background.

Reagan's decision to send American troops to Lebanon would be one of the few major decisions he changed his mind about. Wisely, he pulled the troops out before they became bogged down in a major war. By cutting his losses, relatively little harm was done either to U.S. interests in the Middle East or to Reagan's reputation.

The Decision to Fight
for a Fairer Tax System

*O*NE OF RONALD REAGAN'S MOST important decisions as president was to fight for tax reform. As of 1985, the American tax system was extremely complicated as well as unfair. It was so complicated that an accountant starting out in the business world would have needed 63 feet of bookshelf space for a basic tax library. The tax system was full of loopholes—wording in the law that makes it possible to avoid paying taxes by taking deductions for things such as expensive meals, tickets to ball games, and country club dues. Some people who reported incomes of millions of dollars were paying no taxes at all.

Everybody seemed to think that the tax system was unfair, but almost nobody believed that change

President Ronald Reagan signing the 1986 Tax Reform Act

Donald Regan, Reagan's secretary of the treasury during his first term, talks with the president.

The Department of the Treasury handles the financial affairs of the federal government. The departmental seal, *above,* includes the scales of justice; a key, symbolizing authority; and the year the department was established.

was possible. In 1982 Ronald Reagan had said, "We should go further in reducing tax rates and making the whole system fair and simple for everyone." But one speech supporting a goal is quite different from a major battle to achieve the goal. Why did Ronald Reagan decide on this particular battle?

His interest in tax reform was stimulated by Secretary of the Treasury Donald T. Regan during Reagan's first term. The serious fight for tax reform began toward the end of Reagan's third year as president, when he and his advisers began thinking about the annual State of the Union message. Regan got the president interested by asking him a question. Secretary Regan asked the president what his old employer, General Electric, "had in common with Boeing, General Dynamics, and 57 other big corporations?" Reagan said, "I don't know. What do they have in common?" Regan replied, "Let me tell you, Mr. President, what these outfits have in common is that not one of them pays a penny in taxes to the United States government. Believe it or not, your secretary paid more federal taxes last year than all of these giant corporations put together."

At a meeting a couple of weeks later, the president told Regan that he supported tax reform. He believed strongly in a fair tax system, and he certainly supported lower tax rates. President Reagan never seemed to understand some other parts of his administration's tax proposal—particularly the tax increase that would be placed on businesses—but he stood staunchly behind tax reform and lower income taxes for individuals.

In his 1983 State of the Union speech, Reagan called upon Congress: "Let us go forward with an historic reform for fairness, simplicity, and incentives for growth." He announced that he was asking Secretary of the Treasury Regan to come up with recommendations to simplify the tax code "so that all taxpayers, big and small, are treated more fairly" and to do so by December 1984. Reagan's January

President Reagan traveled across the country, trying to get support for his tax bill. He is in Oshkosh, Wisconsin, *left.*

announcement was not taken seriously at the time, and the senators and representatives in the House chamber broke into laughter. After all, 1984 was an election year. Republicans running for office could use the tax reform promise during their campaigns, but the early November elections would be over before Secretary Regan presented his plan.

Reagan had given the secretary 310 days to come up with a proposal for major reforms in the tax system. The president wanted the new system to raise the same amount of money as the old one, but he did not want the new bill to be a tax increase in disguise. Other than that, he provided no guidance about the shape the reforms should take.

The Treasury Department came up with a plan, which Donald Regan gave to the president on November 26, 1984. Regan once again used an anecdote to explain the new tax plan. The secretary asked Reagan how much he had paid in taxes the year he had made the most money. Reagan said that it was around 50 percent. "Sucker," Regan said. "With the right lawyer and the right accountant and the right tax shelters, you needn't have paid a penny in taxes even if you made more than a million dollars a year—and it would have been perfectly legal and proper."

James Baker was chief of staff during President Reagan's first term in office. At the beginning of the second term, Baker became secretary of the treasury.

The Treasury Department's new plan was criticized by almost every interest group that benefited from any part of the existing tax code—large corporations, labor unions, banks, restaurants, even state and local governments. That criticism, however, did not change Reagan's interest in reform.

Shortly after the Treasury Department proposal was made public, President Reagan named Donald Regan White House chief of staff, and the former chief of staff, James Baker, became secretary of the treasury. Early in 1985, Reagan's advisers were looking for a major issue to present to the Congress. They considered foreign trade and a war on crime, but the president decided to barnstorm around the country trying to sell a somewhat revised version of the Treasury Department's tax proposal.

Reagan spoke in Concord, New Hampshire; Independence, Missouri; and Athens, Tennessee. His speeches followed a question/answer pattern. In Oshkosh, Wisconsin, his speech sounded this way: "Do the people of Oshkosh want our tax system to be complicated and unfair?" The cry came back from the audience, "No!"

"Do you want dramatic simplification that eliminates loopholes and makes our tax system straightforward and fair to all?" "Yes!" The great communicator was striking powerful chords in a nation deeply dissatisfied with its tax system.

An enormous battle broke out in the Congress. Secretary of the Treasury Jim Baker and his staff produced a modified version of the tax reform bill, which Congress finally passed on October 22, 1986. More than any other person, Reagan was responsible for the Tax Reform Act of 1986. The bill dramatically cut personal income tax rates (the top individual tax rate dropped from 50 percent to 28 percent). It took four million of the poorest Americans off the tax rolls and significantly raised taxes on corporations. It also closed loopholes worth 300 billion dollars over a five-year period. Reagan said with some justice, "We got government out of the way and began the process of giving the economy back to the people."

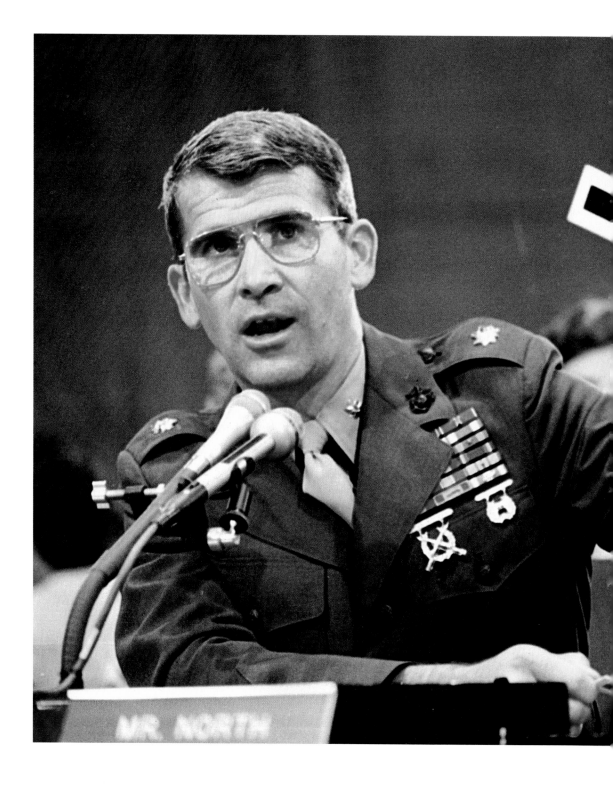

The Iran-contra Affair: The Decision to Trade Arms for Hostages

*T*HE WORST DECISIONS THAT RON-
ald Reagan made as president were those
connected with what is known as the Iran-
contra affair. In the early 1980s, Palestinian terrorists in the Middle East began hijacking commercial
airliners and kidnapping citizens of the United States
and other nations. They wanted to focus attention
on their goal of a Palestinian state and also to get
their cohorts freed from Israeli prisons. Many nations, including the United States, agreed that giving
in to terrorists' demands in order to free hostages
would simply encourage more terrorism. When the

Lieutenant Colonel Oliver North testifies before a joint House-
Senate committee on the Iran-contra affair.

Reagan administration took over, it announced that it would follow the same policy—nothing should be done to reward terrorists for releasing hostages. Publicly, Reagan took a particularly tough stand on this issue in dealing with three nations in the Middle East—Syria, Libya, and Iran—that appeared to be helping terrorist organizations.

Secretly, however, Reagan and his administration did decide to sell U.S. weapons to Iran. How could the United States sell arms in violation of U.S. policy? Furthermore, how could the United States sell arms while Iran was in the middle of a bitter war with Iraq, a war in which the United States claimed neutrality? Reagan gave two reasons for such action. First, he cared very much about getting the release of seven Americans held hostage in Lebanon. Second, some members of the Reagan administration believed that these deals might help improve relations between the United States and Iran, which had been very bitter since the overthrow of the shah. Ayatollah Khomeini, the new leader of Iran, was more than 80 years old, and the United States hoped to have some influence in the country when his successor came to power. However, even if the arms for hostages policy had some merit, it was carried out in a very irresponsible way.

The Reagan administration was never as well organized in foreign affairs as it was in domestic affairs. Except for policy regarding the Soviet Union and Nicaragua (a small country in Central America), Reagan was not that interested in foreign policy. As a result, battles were constantly raging between Secretary of State George Schultz and Secretary of Defense Caspar Weinberger, who frequently disagreed

Ayatollah Khomeini

with each other but got little or no guidance from the president. Inside the White House, Reagan had six different National Security advisers in eight years.

In the summer of 1985, Israel, for its own reasons, suggested that it sell TOWs (tube-launched, optically tracked, wire-guided antitank missiles) and HAWKs (Homing All-the-Way anti-aircraft missiles) to Iran. Israel told the United States that, in return, it expected Iran to pressure terrorist groups to release hostages and that a "private dialogue" on U.S.-Iran relations might develop. Israel wanted U.S. approval of the sale as well as U.S. replacement of the weapons.

Both Secretary Schultz and Secretary Weinberger (who could agree on little else) strongly opposed this

President Reagan asks reporters to stop speculating about hostage negotiations as Nancy Reagan and freed hostage David Jacobsen look on.

From left to right, Donald Regan, President Reagan, Vice President George Bush, former National Security Adviser Robert McFarlane, and his successor Admiral John Poindexter attend a National Security Council meeting.

policy, but President Reagan approved the deal. By doing so, however, the president sacrificed his publicly proclaimed policies in the hope of freeing the hostages. His decision undermined the official U.S. and international policy of not selling arms to Iran. It also violated Reagan's policy of denying weapons to terrorists. Baker, Deaver, and Meese had all left the White House by this time, and the problems with Reagan's decision-making style led to a disaster. Procedures for decision making were so poor in the White House at that time that there was no indication of a formal meeting on the subject or any clear record of when the president approved the plan. Israel delivered a total of 500 missiles to Iran at this time. One hostage was released.

On December 7, 1985, a formal meeting did take place between the president and his advisers about a new and more complicated weapons deal in which additional TOW and HAWK missiles would be sold to Iran. Schultz, Weinberger, and White House chief of staff Donald Regan all opposed the deal, and Weinberger pointed out that there were legal problems with the sale. At a meeting on January 17, 1986, however, Reagan approved the direct sale by the United States of TOW missiles to Iran. Neither Schultz nor Weinberger was present at the meeting. Reagan's decision contradicted U.S. policies of neutrality in the Iran-Iraq war as well as U.S. policy toward dealing with terrorists.

At the same time, the United States was pressing its allies in Europe not to make deals with or sell arms to terrorists. From that point on, U.S. policy involving deals with Iran was handled not by the State Department (which is responsible for foreign relations), nor the Defense Department (which, among other things, is responsible for arms sales to foreign countries), nor even the Central Intelligence Agency (CIA, which handles many secret operations). Instead, deals with Iran were now being handled by members of the National Security Council staff, which is supposed to be no more than an advisory staff on foreign relations for the president. These aides were not only making foreign policy but also carrying it out. They entered into negotiations with Iran to trade arms for hostages.

Oliver North, a marine lieutenant colonel and NSC staff aide, and Richard Secord, a retired U.S. Air Force major general, became the driving force behind the covert (covered over) activities. Mem-

Former Air Force Major General Richard Secord continues his third day of testimony at the Iran-contra hearings.

bers of the NSC staff then dealt with a number of shady characters and private arms dealers, who made huge profits from the sales of missiles to Iran. In February 1986, one thousand TOW missiles were delivered to Iran. Not a single hostage was released!

Although one hostage was released in July 1986, another in September, and yet another in October, three other Americans were taken hostage in Lebanon. Unhappy about the way the policy was going, Oliver North flew to Germany in October 1986, to meet with Ali Hashemi Bahremani, a nephew of Ali Akbar Hashemi Rafsanjani, the speaker of the Iranian parliament. On November 2, 1986, one more hostage was released. The next day the secret was out. *Al-Shiraa,* a Lebanese magazine, published a story about the secret U.S.-Iran negotiations.

America's allies in Europe were appalled when they heard the news. The U. S. Congress was furious.

Soon, another side of the arms for hostages deal began to unravel. Iran had paid three times what the missiles were actually worth. What happened to the millions of dollars netted by the sale of the missiles? Some of the money ended up in the hands of private arms dealers, but much of it ended up with the contras—guerrillas fighting against the pro-Communist government of Nicaragua—in violation of U.S. law.

In 1982, 1984, and 1986, Congress had attempted to ban U.S. assistance to the contras. Congress was afraid the United States would get entangled in another war like the costly one in Vietnam, but Ronald Reagan was a strong supporter of the contras. He called them "freedom fighters," and said they were the "moral equivalent of the Founding

This 11-year-old boy, posing with his automatic weapon in Las Pavas, Nicaragua, says he has been a contra rebel for three years.

Contra rebels north of Jinotega, Nicaragua, contact their military command post, using communication equipment supplied by the United States.

Fathers." Reagan believed the contras were an important part of the worldwide struggle against Communism and therefore entitled to assistance from the United States.

President Reagan met with members of the Tower Commission. The commission's report found Reagan confused and uninformed about Iran-contra dealings.

We do not know what Ronald Reagan knew about the illegal transfer of money from the sale of the missiles in Iran to the Nicaraguan contras. Oliver North arranged the transfers of money. But John Poindexter, North's boss and Reagan's National Security adviser, certainly knew what was going on. We do not know if he told President Reagan, but the scandal dominated the last two years of Reagan's presidency. If Reagan had known about the transfers of money, he would have been condoning a violation of the law—an impeachable offense.

On December 1, 1986, President Reagan appointed a committee called the Tower Board or Tower Commission to review the Iranian arms sales, the diversion of funds to the Nicaraguan rebels, and the role of the National Security Council staff in the overall plan. After 10 weeks of investigation, the commission published a long report. Congressional committees held 40 days of joint public hearings before publishing their report in November 1987.

Nicaragua

*N*icaragua is a small and very poor country—about the size of Alabama—in Central America. Most of its people are farmers who grow cotton, coffee, and sugarcane. For most of its history, Nicaragua has been governed by dictators. From 1912 to 1933, U.S. Marines were stationed in Nicaragua to protect U.S. interests. From 1937 to 1979, members of the Somoza family controlled the Nicaraguan republic. Although U.S. troops were no longer stationed in the country, the United States supported the Somozas, who were strongly anti-Communist. They brought political stability to Nicaragua, but at the price of a cruel and corrupt dictatorship. After a civil war, rebels known as Sandinistas forced Anastasio Somoza Debayle to resign as head of the National Guard and to leave the country.

After Ronald Reagan became president, the United States feared that the Sandinistas were establishing a pro-Communist dictatorship. The United States secretly began to assist a rebel group known as the contras. Some contra leaders had been members of Somoza's National Guard. All during Reagan's presidency, U.S. policy toward Nicaragua was hotly debated. Many U.S. legislators and others thought extended involvement in Central America was not warranted and might actually increase the strife. Reagan, however, was a firm supporter of the contras.

Lawrence Walsh, an Oklahoma attorney who had held positions in the Eisenhower and Nixon administrations, was appointed special prosecutor to investigate further. Eighteen defendants, including North and Poindexter, were convicted or pleaded guilty to various felony charges arising from Walsh's investigation. Some of the convictions, including North's, were overturned on appeal. George Bush pardoned six other convicted defendants after he became president.

When questioned about his role, Reagan did not come out looking good. He appeared to be remote from his administration and confused about the arms deals with Iran and aid to the contras—two issues of great importance to him. He had a difficult time keeping his story straight. After the scandal became public, Reagan first said he had approved the arms shipments to Iran in advance. Then

At a press conference regarding the Iran-contra affair, President Reagan directs reporters' questions to Edward Meese, his press secretary.

Independent counsel Lawrence Walsh investigated the Iran-contra affair for the government. Here, he is arriving at U.S. District Court in Washington, D.C., to attend a session in which former National Security Adviser Robert McFarlane will plead guilty to four charges of withholding information from Congress on aid to Nicaraguan contra rebels.

he said that he had not. Finally, he said he could not remember.

What we can be sure of is that Reagan never disapproved the arms transfer. As president, Reagan was responsible for the policies of his administration and the ways in which those policies were carried out. In the view of the world, the United States appeared hoodwinked by deals in which Iran got thousands of missiles and the United States ended up with a net release of no hostages. President Reagan's integrity and his ability to govern were questioned.

We still cannot be sure of Reagan's involvement in assisting the contras. If he knew what was going on, he broke the law. If he didn't know, he was shockingly ignorant about the conduct of his staff—a staff that had gone out of control.

Either way, both Reagan and the country came out badly. Hostages were still in captivity. Iran had

From top to bottom, former chief of staff Donald Regan, National Security Adviser John Poindexter, Secretary of State George Schultz, and Secretary of Defense Caspar Weinberger testify before the joint congressional committee on the Iran-contra affair.

thousands of missiles. Aid to the contras became even more difficult to attain. Had the procedures for decision making in the White House been better, had policy not been made and carried out in secret, had the president been more curious about what was going on in his administration, had his secretaries of state and defense been kept informed, then such a foreign policy disaster would not have occurred. Indeed, the worst decisions Ronald Reagan made as president were those connected with the Iran-contra affair.

These contra rebels refused to disarm even after United Nations peacekeeping forces arrived in Nicaragua.

CHAPTER TWELVE

The Decision to Seek Arms Reduction Agreements

*I*F REAGAN'S PRESIDENTIAL JUDG-
ment was at its worst during the Iran-contra affair, in no area was it better than in
relations with the former Soviet Union. When
Reagan became president, U.S. relations with the
Soviet Union were more strained than they had been
for almost 20 years. The Soviet Union had invaded
Afghanistan in late 1979. The United States had
not recovered the confidence it had lost during the
Vietnam War, and many Americans felt vulnerable
to what appeared to be a large weapons buildup by
the Soviet Union.

Soviet leader Mikhail Gorbachev and U.S. President Ronald Reagan
shake hands at the end of their first summit meeting in Geneva,
Switzerland.

President Ronald Reagan addressing the British Parliament

Ronald Reagan was a passionate anti-Communist. When he became president, he believed that the Soviet Union could never be trusted to keep an agreement. In his very first news conference, Reagan said that the Soviets were seeking to dominate the world and that they "reserve unto themselves the right to commit any crime, to lie, to cheat, in order to achieve it." In his most celebrated speech about the Soviet Union, which Reagan gave in London on March 8, 1983, the president called the Soviet Union "an evil empire" and "the focus of evil in the modern world."

Far more than most of his advisers, Reagan feared an armed conflict with the Soviet Union. He wanted an arms control agreement, yet he believed that the Soviet Union would not negotiate a reasonable agreement until the United States had greatly strengthened its own military. Thus, Reagan fought for large increases in defense expenditures so the United States could negotiate out of strength. He clearly believed that the Soviets would be unable to increase their own defense expenditures without running the risk of bankruptcy or delaying further the consumer goods the Soviet people wanted. Although Reagan worked for a strong defense, he nevertheless disagreed with the strategy that the best way to preserve the peace was to have two superpowers heavily armed with nuclear weapons.

One of Reagan's important decisions as president was to convince Congress to allocate money for research on a defense system to prevent nuclear missiles from hitting U.S. cities—a screen to knock out nuclear missiles when they came out of the silos. This program, the Strategic Defense Initiative (SDI), nicknamed "Star Wars," was announced to the

In a televised address, President Reagan sought support for his defense budget.

When Ronald Reagan became president, Leonid Brezhnev, *right,* was the leader of the Soviet Union. When Brezhnev died in 1982, Yuri Andropov, head of the Soviet secret police (called the KGB), succeeded him. Because of health problems, Andropov died in January 1984. Konstantin Chernenko succeeded Andropov, but the 73-year-old Chernenko died in March 1985. Reform-minded Mikhail Gorbachev, at the age of 54, replaced him.

nation on March 23, 1983. SDI was Reagan's dream. He was convinced that it could be developed, even when most American politicians and scientists doubted that it could. Most still doubt it.

Reagan had always dreamed of "personally going one-on-one with a Soviet leader because I thought we might be able to accomplish things in our countries diplomats couldn't do because they didn't have the authority." No progress was made in negotiations with the Soviet Union during Reagan's first term, but the situation changed when 54-year-old Mikhail Gorbachev was named secretary of the Communist Party in March 1985.

Gorbachev was aware of the enormous economic problems of his country, many of which were caused by impractical government production plans. The Soviet Union, the largest country in the world—with some of the richest farmland in the world—had to import grain. Meat and sugar, soap and razor

Star Wars

*T*he Strategic Defense Initiative (SDI and sometimes known as "Star Wars") was announced by President Ronald Reagan in March 1983. Reagan strongly supported research and development of an anti-ballistic missile defense system, which would, if it could be developed, make it possible to destroy most incoming Soviet missiles. Such a system would probably have been based in space and would probably have used lasers, particle beams, and powerful computers. Many scientists thought that it was impossible to create such a system. Many others thought it would take decades of work and hundreds of billions of dollars. Reagan, however, believed that such a "peace shield" could be developed to free the whole world from the threat of nuclear destruction.

The Soviet Union strongly attacked the U.S. decision to go ahead with the system. Many Americans and Europeans feared that U.S. support for its development would lead to a renewed arms race.

blades had to be rationed. In an effort to address these problems, Gorbachev established two important policies: sweeping economic reforms *(perestroika)* and open discussion of issues *(glasnost)*. To make these policies succeed, the Soviet Union had to stop spending billions of dollars on arms. Cuts in defense spending, however, required improved relations between the Soviet Union and the United States and its Western European allies. Gorbachev thus began to end Soviet assistance to pro-Communist governments in Asia, Africa, and Latin America. He allowed more freedom for the Soviet people and encouraged the development of private enterprise. He also sought international arms agreements.

A Soviet woman shopper pushes a grocery cart past an almost empty refrigerator and shelves at a food store in Moscow, *right*. *Below*, people wait in line to buy milk.

Reagan was ready. The two men engaged in four summit meetings: in Geneva, Switzerland (November 1985); Reykjavik, Iceland (October 1986); Washington, D.C. (December 1987); and Moscow, Russia (late May and early June 1988).

In the first summit in Geneva, Reagan and Gorbachev established a good working relationship. They spent five hours alone together (along with their interpreters)—part of the time in front of a blazing fire at a boathouse on Geneva's lakeshore. Over dinner Gorbachev seemed to enjoy hearing Reagan's stories about the giant Hollywood film studios of the 1940s. However, the only important agreement at the first summit was an agreement to hold two more meetings.

Reagan and Gorbachev established a good relationship at the first summit in Geneva.

The Reykjavik summit was the most difficult. The meeting took place on short notice (three weeks) at Gorbachev's suggestion. The two men wanted to make enough progress on disarmament so it would be possible to have treaties ready to be signed at the third summit. What appeared to be the agenda for the meeting in Reykjavik was the elimination of intermediate-range missiles from Europe (and maybe Asia) and possibly the elimination of some other nuclear weapons. Unexpectedly, Gorbachev proposed eliminating *all* nuclear weapons of any kind within a 10-year period.

Gorbachev appeared to be willing to drastically cut the number of armed forces his country had in Europe and even permit a way to verify missile cuts. The two men spent almost 10 hours together in face-to-face meetings, alone again except for interpreters. For a while it appeared that they were going to make the greatest arms cuts in history. The sticking point was SDI. Gorbachev insisted that the United States agree not to test it. Reagan refused. He offered to share it with the Soviet Union, if it worked.

Night was falling in Reykjavik on the last day of the meeting. Noting how close they were to an agreement, Reagan asked Gorbachev to "give me this one thing." Gorbachev refused. Reagan says he realized then that Gorbachev had brought him to Iceland with but one purpose—to kill SDI. The president closed his briefing book and stood up. "The meeting is over...," he said. "Let's go, George," Reagan said to Secretary of State George Schultz, who was with him at the time, "we're leaving." Gorbachev was stunned. As Reagan put on his coat, Gorbachev said, "Can't we do something about

The Reagan-Gorbachev meeting in Reykjavik, Iceland, ended in disagreement about Reagan's Strategic Defense Initiative (SDI), nicknamed "Star Wars."

this?" Reagan said, "It's too late." He believed that "SDI held too much potential for the security of mankind to be traded away at the negotiating table."

At the time, it seemed that the summit at Reykjavik had been a disastrous failure, but it wasn't. Although no agreement had been reached to rid the world of nuclear weapons, there had been enough progress toward a treaty on intermediate-range missiles that it could be signed at the next summit. Perhaps Reagan's tough stance allowed Gorbachev to convince other powerful people in the Soviet Union that if they wanted U.S. missiles out of Europe and better relations with the United States, they could not insist on an end to SDI.

When Gorbachev arrived in Washington 14 months later, he said, "Something very serious is afoot, something very profound." The treaty they

Reagan and Gorbachev signed the Intermediate-Range Nuclear Forces (INF) Treaty when they met in Washington in December 1987.

signed provided that each side would destroy all inter-mediate- and shorter-range missiles. Within three years, 859 U.S. and 1,836 Soviet nuclear weapons with a range of from 300 to 3,400 miles would be destroyed.

When Reagan and Gorbachev met again in Moscow six months later, the two countries had already signed an agreement providing for the withdrawal of Soviet troops from Afghanistan. The Moscow meeting symbolized the end of the Cold War.

Perhaps any president serving at the time Gorba-chev came to power would have been wise enough to take advantage of the changes happening in the Soviet Union, but it was Reagan who did it. Whether

The two leaders met again in Moscow in 1988. They are shown here in front of St. Basil's Cathedral in Red Square.

The Cold War

*T*he term *Cold War* is used to describe the intense rivalry that developed between groups of Communist and non-Communist nations after World War II. The struggle was called the Cold War because it did not actually lead to fighting—or "hot" war—on a large scale.

While the United States and the Union of Soviet Socialist Republics (U.S.S.R.) were allies during most of World War II, the two countries were never friendly toward each other. Each country was suspicious of the other. One country was a democracy; the other, a dictatorship. The Soviet Union had suffered terrible losses in the war and believed the U.S. had not done enough to help it. The United States accused the Soviet Union of seeking to expand Communism throughout the world. The Soviet Union accused the U.S. of practicing imperialism and attempting to stop revolutionary activity in other countries. At times these conditions increased the likelihood of a third world war.

After World War II, the U.S. began to withdraw its troops from Europe as fast as possible. But the Soviet Union kept millions of troops in uniform, many of them in small countries near the Soviet Union. Within three years after the end of the war, there were Communist dictatorships in seven Eastern European nations and in the part of Germany occupied by the U.S.S.R. In response, the United States formed the North Atlantic Treaty Alliance (NATO), currently made up of 16 Western nations, to protect Western Europe from Soviet invasion. While the Soviet Union and the United States never fought each other, many small civil wars took place around the world from 1945 into the 1980s. The United States generally supported one side and the Soviet Union the other.

The Cold War came to an end when Mikhail Gorbachev came to power in 1985. To make reforms in the Soviet Union, Gorbachev wanted to reduce spending on defense and attract investment in the Soviet Union by Western nations. By the end of 1990, Communist rule supported by the Soviet Union in Eastern Europe had ended. Free elections were held in almost every East European country, and Germany was unified. In 1991 the Cold War was formally ended when 34 nations met in Paris and signed a treaty in which the United States and the U.S.S.R. agreed to limit the number of troops and weapons each had in Europe.

By 1990 Soviet rule over Eastern Europe had ended. In Berlin, Germany, the wall that had divided the city was torn down. Pieces of the wall became coveted souvenirs.

or not SDI would have been possible, his commitment may have frightened the Soviets enough to get them to the bargaining table. Because of his optimism, because of his self-confidence, because of his likability and great desire to be liked, because he could not be accused of being weak on Communism, and because of his genuine horror of nuclear war, he was exceptionally well suited to deal with Gorbachev. As Reagan later wrote, "For the eight years I was president I never let my dream of a nuclear-free world fade from my mind."

INF Treaty On-Site Inspections:
A Status Report

*T*he Intermediate-Range Nuclear Forces (INF) Treaty between the United States and the former Soviet Union entered into force on June 1, 1988, when President Reagan and Soviet General Secretary Gorbachev exchanged the articles of implementation at the Moscow Summit. The treaty called for the elimination of all U.S. and Soviet ground-launched missile systems with the range of 500 to 5,500 kilometers (about 300 to 3,400 miles) within three years after entry into force. As a result, members of the On-Site Inspection Agency (OSIA) have witnessed the elimination of an entire class of U.S. and Soviet intermediate-range missiles.

Since July 1, 1988, inspectors from the On-Site Inspection Agency have conducted 452 baseline, elimination, quota, and closeout inspections, and maintained a continuous-monitoring presence at the former SS-20/23 final assembly plant in Votkinsk, Russia. In the same period, OSIA escorted 270 foreign inspector teams at U.S. sites in this country and Western Europe while also conducting the escort function at the Russian continuous-monitoring facility in Magna, Utah.

The On-Site Inspection Agency is responsible for conducting and coordinating the treaty's inspection provisions. For the first time in U.S. and Soviet history, on-site inspections were included in the verification process of an arms control agreement between these nations.

The first three years of the treaty were marked by an almost continuous elimination of missiles, launchers, and related equipment. Beginning with the first Soviet SS-12 missile destruction at Saryozek in August 1988, U.S. inspectors witnessed the elimination of 1,846 Soviet missiles through May 12, 1991. Since the first elimination of a Pershing 1-A missile at Longhorn Army Ammunition Plant near Marshall, Texas, on September 8, 1988, Soviet inspectors viewed the destruction of the 846 U.S. missiles.

All declared shorter-range INF systems, those with ranges from 500 to 1,000 kilometers, were eliminated one month in advance of the treaty deadline of November 30, 1989. The U.S. Pershing 1-A was the first shorter-range system to be completely eliminated, with the final missile eliminated on July 6, 1989. The Soviet Union eliminated the last of its declared shorter-range missiles, the SS-12 on July 26 and the SS-23 on October 27, 1989.

The United States eliminated its last ground-launched cruise missile on May 1, 1991. The last Pershing II was destroyed on May 6, 1991. The Soviet Union destroyed the last of 80 SSC-X-4 nondeployed cruise missiles on October 5, 1988, and the last of six SS-5s on August 16, 1989. With the destruction of the last declared SS-4 on May 22, 1990, the only remaining Soviet intermediate-range system enumerated in the treaty was the SS-20 until its final elimination on May 12, 1991.

Continuous portal monitoring began in both countries in July 1988. At Magna, Utah, and Votkinsk, Russia, permanent communities of up to 30 inspectors each are located outside the gates of former INF missile production and final assembly plants to check existing vehicles for treaty-limited items. These monitoring operations may continue inspections to 2001. Continuous portal monitoring operations at Votkinsk and Magna are proceeding with rotations of portal inspectors occurring at three week and monthly intervals, respectively.

The breakup of the Soviet Union and the formation of the Commonwealth of Independent States on January 1, 1992, has not impacted INF inspections or continuous portal monitoring operations. A significant change, however, has been the establishment of three additional Points-of-Entry (POEs) for inspection teams. The POEs, locations where inspectors enter the sovereign territory of an INF treaty party, were established to permit access to inspectable sites. In addition to the two original sites, Moscow and Ulan-Ude, Russia, the following locations are now official INF POEs: Minsk, Belarus; Almaty, Kazakhstan; and Kiev, Ukraine.

Quota or short-notice inspections of formerly declared facilities are proceeding. The inspections help maintain confidence that both parties are complying with the terms of the treaty. The treaty provided for 20 quota inspections per year for the first three years. The inspections will continue at the rate of 15 per treaty year through May 1996, and at a rate of 10 per treaty year from June 1, 1996, through June 1, 2001.

Soviet Major Igor Kirichenko and American Lieutenant Colonol Vitali Mostovoj are conducting an INF baseline inspection to confirm the numbers of missiles counted at Saryozek in the former USSR. The representative of the visiting country verifies the number of missiles in the host country.

U.S. and Soviet/Russian INF Inspections and Eliminations (As of June 1994)

Inspections

	Soviet/Russian Inspectors at U.S. Sites	U.S. Inspections at Former Soviet Sites
Continuous Monitoring:	279	290
Elimination:	109	137
Quota:	105	105
Closeout:	27	100
Baseline:	34	117
Total:	554	749

Completed Eliminations

	Missiles Subject to Elimination*	Missiles Eliminated	
Soviet Systems			
SS-20	654	ELIMINATED	654
SS-12	718	ELIMINATED	718
SS-23	239	ELIMINATED	239
SS-4	149	ELIMINATED	149
SS-5	6	ELIMINATED	6
SSC-X-4	80	ELIMINATED	80
Total	1,846		1,846
U.S. Systems			
Pershing IA	169	ELIMINATED	169
Pershing II	234	ELIMINATED	234
GLCM	443	ELIMINATED	443
Total	846		846

*Source: INF Treaty Memorandum of Understanding, 1 June 1988 Update

The Reagan Presidency

*W*AS RONALD REAGAN A GREAT president, a good president, or a poor president? It is much too early to judge fairly. Only a few presidents since Washington have left office as popular as Reagan after two full terms in office.

Reagan seemed to know much less and work much less than most presidents. This became especially evident during the Iran-contra affair. His policy of high military spending and tax cuts left the United States a dangerously large deficit. His administration's failure to regulate the savings and loan industry may cost taxpayers one trillion dollars. During the Reagan administration, serious scandals occurred in the Pentagon and in the Department of Housing and Urban Development.

Ronald Reagan prepares to give his farewell address as president.

President Reagan shakes hands with President-elect George Bush before leaving for the Capitol for Bush's inauguration as the 41st president.

Yet for most of Reagan's presidency, the economy boomed. Congress passed the most dramatic tax reform in American history. To a large extent, Reagan restored national self-confidence by transferring his own confidence in America to his fellow citizens. Perhaps most important, Reagan's defense and foreign policies helped make the world a safer place.

On his last day in the White House, Reagan heard his last report from the man who was then his National Security adviser, General Colin Powell. Powell told him, "The world is quiet today, Mr. President." Reagan then sat down and wrote a letter to George Bush, telling him "to carry on and walk with God." He gazed at the Rose Garden of the White House, where he had enjoyed feeding the squirrels. He and Nancy Reagan walked through all the rooms of the family quarters of the White House. They walked down the central hallway and stood on what is known as the Truman balcony, looking toward the Jefferson Memorial. A little after 11:00 A.M., the 77-year-old president, in a black topcoat and white silk scarf, got into a limousine with George Bush and rode to the Capitol. "Hail to the Chief," the presidential march, was played in his honor one more time, as he walked down the steps to his seat.

In his inaugural address, George Bush spoke of Reagan as a man "who earned a lasting place in our history." At 12:50 P.M. President and Mrs. Bush escorted the Reagans to a helicopter on the grounds of the Capitol. The two men exchanged salutes. The helicopter lifted off, swooped down over the Capitol, and circled it twice. As they flew over the White House, the ex-president said to his wife, "There's our little cottage." From there they went on to Andrews Air Force Base, then to Los Angeles and retirement.

A few days before, Reagan had given a farewell speech. This is part of what he said:

> I've spoken of the shining city all my political life, but I didn't know if I ever communicated what I saw when I said it. But it in my mind was a tall, proud city built on rocks stronger than oceans, windswept, Godblessed, and teeming with people of all kinds living in harmony and peace...
>
> And she's still a beacon, still a magnet for all who must have freedom, for all the pilgrims from all the lost places who are hurtling through the darkness, toward home...
>
> And so, good-bye.

After Bush's inaugural ceremony, the Reagans walked to the helicopter waiting for them on the grounds of the Capitol.

Index

Acknowledgments

Mead Art Museum, Amherst College, 8; AP/Wide World, 23, 26 (both), 34-35, 36, 37, 41, 72-73, 76, 77 (sidebar), 78, 79, 86-87, 88, 92, 93, 97, 98 (all), 99, 104, 106, 113, 120; Jeff Greenberg, 106 (bottom); Hollywood Book and Poster, 22 (both), 25, 57 (sidebar); Jim Hubbard, 67; Hunt Oil Co./Lynn Abercrombie, 38 (sidebar); Independence National Historical Park, 6-7; Independent Picture Service, 82 (sidebar); Library of Congress, 9, 55; Minneapolis Public Library Picture Collection, 59 (bottom sidebar); National Aeronautics and Space Administration (NASA), 48 (sidebar); National Republican Party, 59 (top sidebar); On-Site Inspection Agency, Department of Defense, 116; Ronald Reagan Home Preservation Foundation, Dixon, Illinois, 18-19; Courtesy Ronald Reagan Library, 2-3, 12, 14, 16, 17, 20 (both), 21 (both), 24, 27 (sidebar), 28-29, 30, 31 (both), 32 42-43, 44 (both), 48, 49 (left), 50 (both), 52-53, 54, 56, 57 (left), 58 (both), 59 60, 61, 62-63, 64, 71, 75, 80-81, 82, 83, 90, 94, 96, 102, 103, 107, 109, 110, 111, 118, 121; UPI/Bettmann, 38, 46-47, 68 (sidebar), 84, 89, 91 (sidebar), 100-101; Bill Fitz-Patrick/The White House, 15; White House, 55.

About the Author

Jeffrey B. Morris authored the Great Presidential Decisions series, first conceived by his historian father, the late Richard B. Morris. He coauthored the *Encyclopedia of American History* with his father and thinks "writing children's books is a very important thing for a scholar to do."

Jeffrey Morris attended Princeton University and received his law degree and his Ph.D. in political science from Columbia University, where he later served as an administrator. He taught American government at the University of Pennsylvania, where he won the highest award for distinguished teaching. Morris also was a visiting professor at Brooklyn Law School. He served as chief research associate to Chief Justice Warren Burger in his role as head of the federal court system. Morris has traveled in Africa and Central and South America, and he has lectured in Europe. He is currently a professor at Touro Law School in Huntington, New York, where he teaches law and legal history.

He is married to Dona Baron Morris. They have two children, David and Deborah, and two cats, Sweet Pea and Smokey.

The Washington Way
The Jefferson Way
The Lincoln Way
The FDR Way
The Truman Way
The Reagan Way